The viking assaut on Europe

From the very onset of their exactions, during the last decade of the 8th Century, the Vikings earned themselves the reputation of goldthirsty and bloodthirsty pirates; a portrait that the clerics were only too happy to blacken... Medieval chroniclers were later to take pleasure in relating their acts of vandalism, pillaging and brutality of all sorts. In the 19th Century, the Romantics preferred to depict the more buoyant image of the longships, the sea, adventure, ferocity and bravery, finally symbolising the superiority of a race; and our contemporaries have inherited a multi-facet vision of the Viking ranging from the satanic barbarian to the regenerating hero. For the legend is steadfast and our imagination delights in it: for several centuries, the Western world was unaware of the rich cultural heritage of ancient Scandinavia where, for over two hundred years, men took to the sea to bathe Europe in blood and fire. But the "Viking phenomenon" would never have persisted so long had they been simple bloodthirsty predators. This phenomenon is, in fact, the emanation of a well-established society whose political and cultural upsurge was to leave its mark on entire Europe.

The Norwegians, sailing west, braved the ocean towards the Western Isles of Scotland and Ireland, then the Faeroe Islands and Iceland before reaching Greenland and even the American coast. The Danes attacked the French Empire and, crossing the North Sea, reached England. The Swedes, also known as Varegs, followed the course of the Great Russian Rivers to the banks of the Black and the Caspian Seas. Commerce was one of the great pacific activities of ancient Scandinavia whose trading posts often attracted numerous foreign merchants. Commerce blossomed after the 9th Century and followed, as the Viking expansion had, the road east passing the two great caravan routes from the Far East.

From one end of Europe to the other, the Vikings created a great mixing of populations. The Irish identified with and drew close to their Norwegian invaders, whom many followed as far as Iceland (often as slaves). In England, the Danes were firmly established, particularly in Yorkshire, whilst in Normandy, integration was rapid with the marriage of many Vikings to Frankish women. Their linguistic contribution to European languages reflects the excellent socio-cultural mark they left: taking into account the lexical erosion over the centuries, the remains of Norman dialect are impressive and quite surprising.

The Vikings arrived in Europe with their own know-how, but they readily sought inspiration in all that they discovered throughout their travels. The Irish, who were ahead of them in the literary field, influenced the poetry of Norwegian skalds as early as the 9th Century, and even Old Norse prose in Iceland, in the 11th Century. The mixing of Celtic and Nordic cultures reached its peak on the Isle of Man, as illustrated on funeral steles and crosses adorned with both oghams and runes, Christian and Pagan motifs, Gaelic and Norse names. However, the most impressive domain remains naval construction: the Vikings taught ship-building to both Celts and Franks, thus perpetuating their techniques well beyond their integration.

To say that the Vikings modelled the European map is far from an exaggeration. Whilst the Orkneys traversed over two centuries of political intensity, in Iceland, the masterpiece of the Viking adventure, a most original nation was blooming. The Vikings gave a boost to the Irish economy, contributed towards the uniting of Anglo-Saxon England, made true capitals of Dublin and London, and rejuvenated Normandy whilst preserving the Carolingian system in force. Today, the Isle of Man can be proud of hosting the oldest parliamentary assembly in Europe, the *Tynwald*, which, since its institution by the Vikings, has never encountered the slightest interruption.

In other words, a certain common cultural context has developed or reinforced the inheritance of the "Norsemen", which remains present, in one way or another, in most of Europe. Originating from the European outskirts, they were the initiators of a genuine modernity which remains evident today.

Jean RENAUD
Professor at the University of Caen

Gissur defying the Huns,
Peter Nicolaï Arbo (1831-1892),
oil on canvas, 1886.
Nasjonalgalleriet, Oslo, Norway.

northern pirates and saxons

When the very first Viking incursions took place, at the end of the 8th Century, in Lindisfarne in England, on the Isle of Iona off the Scottish coast and on the Irish shores, the Franks and the Saxons, all "Northern Barbarians", were already familiar with the road to these poorly defended lands. Between the German pirates evoked by Tacitus in the 1st Century AD, and the Saxon invaders described by the Venerable Bede at the beginning of the 8th Century, the likeness is striking: violent and surprise attacks, unequalled navigation techniques, shape and manoeuvrability of ships, etc.; so many indicators of the Viking raids. However, not only piracy was involved: the Germans and Scandinavians regularly took the commercial trading route linking the North-East of England and the mouth of the Rhine. In Brittany and in Normandy too, the presence of Saxon pirates as early as the 6th Century has been confirmed by archaeologists. By embarking and sailing towards Britain, Brittany and Normandy, the Vikings followed a maritime route which was already well-known to the Germanic population – but this in no way minimises their audacity or the prowess of their ships. And they did so with the full knowledge of the military and political resources and weaknesses of the kingdoms they were preparing to conquer, before taking root there and often changing the course of history.

Viking warrior,
Lithography, 9th Century.

Decorated spoon, Merovingian period. Musée d'Aquitaine, Bordeaux.

Sword, Kindby's Tomb 1 7th Century. National Museum of Denmark, Copenhagen.

Tortoise-shaped brooches National Museum of Denmark, Copenhagen.

The influence of geography on human destiny? The explanation whereby a sudden overpopulation is accounted for by the no less sudden and vigorous Viking outbreak on the Western European seas remains highly debated. Indeed, a glimpse at the map of Norway reveals the development limits that the agricultural population must have met with.

However, the extent to which geography conditioned the different routes chosen from Scandinavian countries throughout the Viking adventure is unquestionable, even when taking into account the uncertainty of the names given to these northern adventurers by the clerics of invaded territories. Norwegians, Danes and Swedes did not travel by the same route. The majority of Norwegians ventured west, either to Great Britain and its Isles, or to other undiscovered territories in the Far West. The Danes also chose to travel towards Great Britain and France, territories whose destiny was to be largely modified by their presence; whilst the Swedes, neighbours of the Baltic Sea, turned east towards the future Baltic States, Russia yet to be invented, and Finland whose Kings married the most beautiful girls, according to the chroniclers.

Sigtuna's Viking, bone.
Sigtuna Museum, Sweden.

Dragon ship,
Anglo-Saxon manuscript,
10th Century
British Museum, London.

*Ancient Scandinavia, engraving by Antonio Lafreri (1512-1577), detail of the **Carta Marina Olaus Magnus**, 1572.*

gods, men and destiny

The Vikings, and more generally speaking, the ancient Scandinavians, practised a religion that was not based on a cult of strength, war or death, but founded on notions of fertility and fecundity with religious practices where magic played an essential role. As far as we know, this religion was linked to the great forces of nature to which the Scandinavian gods bear witness: Sól (Sun), Ægir (Ocean), Jörð (Earth) or Þórr [Thor] (Thunder).

Silver Þórr hammer, Romersdal. National Museum of Denmark, Copenhagen.

Among the great gods of the Scandinavian pantheon, are Týr, guarantor of worldly order, Þórr, the popular destroyer of giants, Baldr, the handsome, the good, the young warrior, representing all that is stability, righteousness, integrity. The forces of disorder opposed them, such as Surtr and, in particular the seductive representative of evil, Loki, who was responsible for the death of Baldr during the Battle of Ragnarök (*Doom of the Gods*) and end of the world. Science, black magic and poetry were reunited and personified in d'Óðinn [Odin], the one-eyed god, initiated to the secrets of the world at the foot of the world tree Yggdrasill, and the master of the Valkyries, who read destiny and presided over sacrifices. Finally, those who watched over fecundity were split into two families: the Vanes, among whom we find the Freyr-Freyja couple who were divinities of pleasure and happiness; and opposed to them, the Ases, Skaði and Hel who reigned over the world of the dead and who guaranteed the fertility of the Earth and all that grew there.

Jet-black amulet. Gripping beast. Bergen University Museum, Norway.

Among Indo-European religions, the Scandinavian, and therefore Viking religion was one of those which left little trace: no temples, but natural sanctuaries, no clergy,

Thor fighting against the giants, *Marten Eskil Winge. Oil on canvas, 1872.*

Pendants (Valkyrie), silver, Kalmergården-Tissø. National Museum of Denmark, Copenhagen.

not even words to render the notion of prayer or adoration, very few rites and even less dogma. The Vikings sacrificed to their gods in exchange for their protection, and they expected a just return for the gifts they gave. But above all, the key element of the Viking's relationship with the supernatural concerned destiny, a destiny that the Vikings sought through magic, through the reading of the Runes, and that they readily accepted with neither complaint nor trickery, when they discovered their fate.

society

Scandinavian society during the Viking era comprised two major categories, slaves and free men, and was based on two fundamental units: family, in the largest sense of the term "household", and all that aims at rendering the family community autonomous within a poor environment and hostile conditions.

Two black ceramics, clay, Gotland Museum, Visby, Sweden.

The *bóndi* (pl. *bœndr*), free man and land-owner, was an essential constituent of society, and was in charge of affairs and private cult. He could be a merchant, a sailor or a warrior. The *bœndr*, as members of the assembly, together with the *þing*, who chose the king, benefited from significant power and a great liberty of expression. They also had authority over the *hreppr*, a solidarity fund aimed at helping the poor, the aged and victims of catastrophes of all sorts. Slaves were an integral part of Scandinavian society. They were included in the family circle and often had the opportunity of buying back their freedom.

Konungr (pl. *konungar*), the king, exerted his power on the community that had chosen and enthroned him on a sacred stone, thus becoming the guardian of the Earth and guarantor of its fecundity. He did not exert absolute sovereignty and often submitted himself to the law dictated by the *þing*. He did not charge taxes and lived from his private revenue and that of the royal domain.

Meat fork, iron, Västmanland, Dingtuna. Statens Historiska Museum, Stockholm, Sweden.

In ancient Scandinavian religion, the *goði* was a sacrificing priest embodying the spiritual authority in a given community. However, he did not belong to an institutional and hierar-chical priestly order. Christian priests and monks arrived during the last period of the Viking epic, and their hold on society was to be far more stringent.

Free women (those who were not slaves) were legally inferior to men and expected to yield to their decisions. However, many sagas highlight the vigorous and independent nature of Scandinavian women. While their husbands left to fish, hunt, trade and fight, Scandinavian women assumed the entire charge of the family domain. Even after marriage, they kept their dowry, and could divorce should they consider their husband to be unworthy, or should they be insulted or beaten. Women took part in the most far-fetched Viking adventures such as that of Vinland, however only in small numbers, since Viking men were glad to take wives and concubines among the local population.

Bronze bowl (scales), Rogaland, Norway. Bergen University Museum, Norway.

Bowl with steatite handle. Bergen University Museum, Norway.

the long history of the runes

Runic writing is generally considered to belong to the Vikings, since the Vikings were those who exploited it in the most remarkable way. However, the runic alphabet, or 24 sign *fuþark* (name derived from it first 6 letters), was very probably born in Northern Italy towards the end of the 1st Century BC, and was later to migrate towards Germanic and Scandinavian countries in the 2nd and 3rd Centuries AD. Runic writing was, at its outset, based on cult: the runic engraver was initiated and, through his art, he was linked to occult powers. The formulae engraved on arms (sword handles, spearheads) were supposed to endow them with a supernatural force, and they transformed jewels (fibulas, bracteates) into talismans and amulets.

Runic stone. Sigtuna Museum.

The Runes remained, until the 7th Century, the only script used by the Germanic population, some of whom exported it to Christian England, where Latin script had, however, existed for many hundreds of years. Accustomed to the progression of their language and dialect, the Anglo-Saxons created a 28 sign runic sequence at the beginning of the 7th Century: the Anglo-Saxon *fuþorc*.

In Scandinavia, following the great phonetic transformations leading to Norse, the Viking language, *fuþark* became insufficient and engravers could no longer practise their art – until an unbelievable restoration of the tradition at the beginning of the 9th Century. Texts became longer and took on an increasingly secular nature and, even if the traditional mediums (metal, wood, bone) subsisted, stone became the most frequently used. But the most astonishing change was that the new *fuþark* contained only 16 signs, quite an exceptional reduction in the history of scripts.

Rune engraved bones. Sigtuna Museum.

Above:
Harp key engraved with Runes. Sigtuna Museum.

The spread of Runic script in Scandinavia, then throughout the entire geographical area covered by the Vikings, from Greenland to the Ukraine, has resulted in some 700 inscriptions currently observed in Denmark, 900 in Norway and 3,200 in Sweden. The western colonies have 200, but not one single inscription is noted in Normandy! Most of the inscriptions were made on raised stones to honour the memory of a family member or a friend. The Jelling stones (in Denmark), dating from the 10th Century, are among the most famous of all runic stones, the smallest of which was erected by King Gormr in memory of his spouse. Their son Haraldr Bluetooth had the most impressive and magnificently decorated stone erected, on which he recalled his reign over Denmark and Norway and his conversion of the Danish to Christianity.

Even if Latin script, reserved to parchment, had cohabited over a long period with runes engraved on other mediums, runic inscriptions breathed their ultimate breath at the beginning of the 14th Century. In a Scanian monastery, runes (known as "pointed runes" becoming a complete 23 sign "alphabet") were still used to copy the Scania Law (*Codex runicus*) onto parchment in the early 1300's, however, the epigraphic tradition of Scandinavian Runes finally came to an end. Only a few rare remnants exist.

Great Jelling Stone, Denmark.

viking art

Viking art is part of a long-lasting tradition which, since the Stone Age, has combined animal representation and a virtuoso stylisation of motifs leading to apparent abstraction. This tradition thrived during the Viking era, and was inspired by many foreign stimuli. Rather than Viking Art, one should really refer to it as virtuoso craftsmanship. Beauty and usefulness were indissociable, be it in the creation of objects for daily use, for combat, for ceremonies, or for those representing sacrifice or commemoration. The presence, in the Scandinavian pantheon, of Völundr, a marvellous craftsman and master blacksmith of all mediums, is therefore in no way fortuitous.

Weathervane, copper, Hälsingland, Söderala. Statens Historiska Museum, Stockholm, Sweden.

Accompanying a very limited representation of vegetation, animals are omnipresent, almost intrusive, in all styles of Viking art, with, as a leitmotiv, "gripping beasts": vigorous, stylised and sinuous animals, clinging to one another, or to the frame of the object they adorn.

The first art style of the Viking era was that of Oseberg in Norway, or Broa in Sweden, where barely recognisable animals were inextricably mingled. The style founded in Borre, in Norway, offered the most fantastic examples of work on metal, gold and silver reuniting, in particular, filigree, granulation and niello work. In the Danish style, from Mammen, animals were less stylised, their bodies were adorned with dotted work, and swirls and leaves appeared.

Spiral silver bracelet, two silver Permian rings. National Museum of Denmark, Copenhagen.

The royal Danish site of Jelling, also gave its name to a more airy style of art, in which the ribboned bodies of animals intertwined and arched over each other.

Harness bow with animal heads, gilded bronze, Søllested. National Museum of Denmark, Copenhagen.

The Ringerike style, famous for its finely worked metal weathervanes and historiated stones, appeared at the beginning of the 11th Century.

Chain with zoomorphic extremities,
silver, Mandemark.
National Museum of Denmark, Copenhagen.

gold and silver

During the entire Viking era, silver remained the most sought after metal, not only for jewellery, but chiefly as the foundation of the monetary system which was always based on pure metal weight. The beauty of a silver object, be it stolen or exchanged, would not prevent it from being melted into ingots or bars, which themselves would then be cut and weighed on the folding scales that any worthy Viking always carried with him. Neither gold, the metal of gods and kings, so admirably worked during the 6th and 7th Centuries, nor silver was not to be found in a crude state in Scandinavian countries. The Vikings obtained their precious metal from different regions, which varied depending on the political climate and war. The East, including the Far East and Russia, was the main supplier up to the year 850 AD, date at which the Arabs closed the traditional trading routes; trading with the East was only to resume a century later, and via other itineraries. In the 9th and 11th Centuries, silver came from Germany, mainly thanks to commerce. During the 10th Century, it was Great Britain that endowed the Vikings, first of all with silver extorted for taxes and duties, the *danegeld* among others, then thanks to the pay of soldiers serving the Viking kings: before becoming King Canute, the Dane Knútr paid his men with English coins.

And finally, the Urnes style, named after sculptures in the Urnes stave church in Norway, stretches Viking art to its very limits, filling the entire space with swirls of vegetation and twisted stylised animals.

But beyond these Viking styles, these adornments that transfigure the most ordinary of objects: Danish ear pick or Finish ski, the summit of Viking art is to be found in naval construction, the finest examples of which are the Skuldelev

Three filigree pendants, silver, Terslev. National Museum of Denmark, Copenhagen.

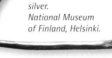

Pennanular brooch, silver. National Museum of Finland, Helsinki.

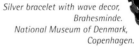

Silver bracelet with wave decor, Brahesminde. National Museum of Denmark, Copenhagen.

Silver and ceramic treasure from Hägvalds in Gerum. Gotland Museum, Visby, Sweden.

The sea wrapped in sails

On the 8th of June 793, the Vikings made their thunderous entry into European history, by attacking the monastery on the Holy Island of Lindisfarne, on the north-western coast of England. From then on, those who were called the Danes or the Normans, launched raids on the English, Breton and French coasts in order to gain honour and riches on the seas. And riches they obtained. Their assaults aroused great horror, all the more fervent since they attacked the most sacred of places: churches, monasteries and their treasures. As the last of Europe's Pagans, the notion of sacrilege did not even cross their minds, but the clerics who related their exactions portrayed them as monsters vomited from Hell.

Their fleets, although in reality in fewer numbers than reported by the chroniclers, attacked towns and cities, by sailing up the water courses. In charge of the fleets were famous leaders such as Ragnarr Hairy-Breeches, Hásteinn [Hasting] and Ívarr. The Vikings settled near to rivers or coasts, and on islands such as Noirmoutiers in France, Thanet near London or Jeufosse on the River Seine, and awaited the best time to attack. They appeared in the Seine Bay in 820, Rouen was ravaged in 841, and Nantes in 843. They

Norman pirates in the 9th Century, *Évariste Vital Luminais, 1822-1896. Museum of Art and Archeology, Moulins.*

besieged Paris in 845 and Charles the Bald paid a heavy tribute to ensure that they cease their attacks on the city and leave. Also around 845, the Vikings attacked south-western France, before heading for Spain, Portugal and the Mediterranean. Throughout the 9th Century, they employed the same stratagem based on rapid and surprise attacks enabling them to take possession of the most precious goods on site, before fleeing, sometimes after having set fire to their target.

Viking ships were the essential constituent of their success. Thanks to their surprising perfection, they were long to be known as the kings of

Construction of a boat, illustration from **Historia de Gentibus Septentrionalibus** *by Olaus Magnus (1490-1558), engraved wood, 16th Century. British Library, London.*

*Knight,
piece of a morse ivory chess set
(9th Century),
Isle of Lewis, Outer Hebrides, Scotland.
National Museum of Scotland, Edinburgh.*

*Illustration from **The History of France** by Michelet, engraving.*

*The warrior and the **berserkr**,
pieces of a morse ivory chess set
(9th Century), Isle of Lewis,
Outer Hebrides, Scotland.
National Museum of Scotland, Edinburgh.*

the seas. The Viking ship, or *langskip* (longship), a long warship, the *knörr*, a mixed vessel trans- porting men and their equipment, and the *snekkja*, or *skeið*, are all the product of several centuries of naval construction. The 23 metre long Nydam Boat, built as early as the 4th Century, is an excellent illustration. Several masterpieces have been dug out of the blue clay in Oseberg and Gokstad in Norway, or dragged from the depths of the Roskilde Fjord in Skuldelev. Designed for coastal navigation, the high seas, trading, war or fishing, all of these ships comprised, over and above their differing shapes depending on their intended use, the same characteristics. Clinker built, sail-pro- pelled or rowboats, very shallow with a folding mast, they were light enough to be dragged along the beaches and rapidly set afloat, or even carried during inland incursions. Raid victims highlighted the terrifying appearance of the painted and gilded dragons that adorned their bows, hence the name "drakkar", or dragon vessel, used by Auguste Jal in 1839.

Over several decades after the Lindisfarne attack, the Vikings continued to torment England. The pressure they exerted was ever increasing when they settled on the Isle of Thanet, at the mouth of the Thames in 850, and took hold of London and Canterbury. In 860, the inhabitants of Kent started to pay the *danegeld* tribute so that the Vikings would leave them in peace. Before the end of the 9th Century, the Vikings, having established the Great Army, assigned themselves the *Danelaw*: the entire land to the east of a boundary running from London to Chester. The Scandinavian conquest came to an end in 954, upon the death of the king Eiríkr Bloodaxe. England was to see its political structure transformed from a divided to a unified kingdom.

The 8th Century also saw Norwegian Vikings settle in the north-east of Scotland, and in the Shetlands and the Orkneys where they proclaimed themselves Counts. From there, they continued on to the Isle of Man. The immi- nent danger led the Scots to reunite: Kenneth MacAlpin created the first kingdom of Scotland together with the Scots from Ireland and the indigenous Pictish tribes. On the Irish coast, the Vikings established colonies and created towns, among which Dublin emerged. In 874, Ívarr, one of the leaders of the Great Army, was considered to be "king of the Northmen of all Ireland and Britain". Despite the Battle of Clontarf in 1014, won by the Irish King Brian Boru, the kingdom of Dublin which had been founded by Ívarr was to persevere until 1052.

*Viking sword, wrought iron,
Loire, Nantes, Isle of Bièce,
9th Century.
Dobrée Museum, Nantes.*

*Viking sword, wrought iron,
pommel inlaid with silver,
Loire, Nantes, Isle of Bièce,
9th Century.
Dobrée Museum, Nantes.*

*Scale model of the
Gokstad boat
(Norway),
wood, rivet assembly.
Museum of Terre-Neuvas
and deep sea fishing,
Fécamp.*

*War axe, Runnymede.
Late Saxon.
Museum of London.*

*Arrowheads, iron.
National Museum of Finland, Helsinki.*

The quest for new territories

After the raids, the Vikings entered into a period of colonisation which was to last the entire 10th Century. Their settling in England, in the *Danelaw*, around the town that the Danish renamed Jórvík [York], in Ireland or in the Northern Scottish Isles has already been mentioned. They continued thus to the East, creating Russia. This great expedition in the quest of new territories took on many forms varying from negotiation to high sea adventure.

The Norwegians were those who transpired to be the most fervent of new land hunters. After having settled in the Scottish archipelagos, and having established a small farming community in the Faeroe Islands, several adventurers reported the existence of a large island, that Raven-Flóki named *Ísland* ("land of ice"), an island that sheltered only a few Irish hermits. Tradition claims that Ingólfr Arnarson was the first to settle on the island in 874, shortly to be followed by some 400 colonists whose names are mentioned in the *Landnámabók*, the Book of Settlements. The population was reinforced with the arrival of Irish citizens (and in particular of Irish women) captured during the raids on the Green Isle. Iceland had the remarkable originality of being governed by a parliament (*alþing*) comprised of the island's free men, seeing no necessity to establish any form of royal institution – until such times as the king of Norway took over the island in the 13th Century.

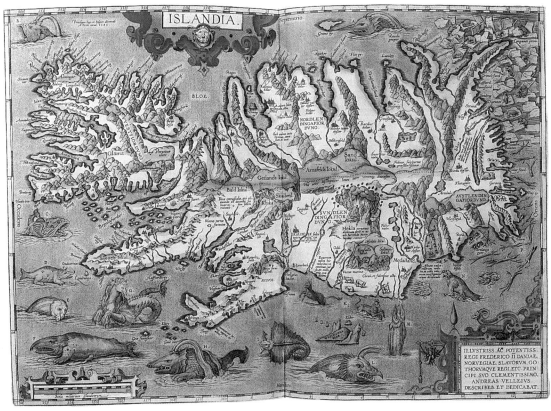

Map of Iceland, by Abraham Ortel Ortelis (1585).
Royal Geographical Society, London.

The First Cargo, *N.C. Wyeth, oil on canvas, 1910.*
New York Public Library.

A century or so after the colonisation of Iceland, around 985, Erik the Red, who was banished from the island, set out to conquer new territories. He discovered a land that he was to name *Grœnland* ("green land") to honour its verdant features. A few Icelanders emigrated to Greenland with him, but the terrible conditions there were to lead to the total extinction of this small colony in the 16th Century. Erik the Red's son, Leifr Eriksson ("Leif the Lucky") in turn set out on expedition in the North Atlantic in 999 AD. He was searching for the land that his compatriot, Bjarni Herjólfsson, had previously perceived, after going astray off the coast of Greenland. Leifr hugged the shores of two lands that he named Helluland and Markland, before arriving at Vinland where, vines were said to grow.

And it was hence that Leif the Lucky discovered the shores of North America, and specifically those of Labrador and Newfoundland, where he settled temporarily. Other expeditions were to follow, in particular that of Þorfinnr Karlsefni, without giving way to any genuine colonisation. The discovery, in 1959, of remains of Scandinavian type settlements in L'Anse-aux-Meadows in Newfoundland would appear to confirm the Viking colonisation in this area.

Thingbrekka, Thingvellir, *William Collingwood,*
(1819-1903). British Museum.

And they founded Normandy

On the death of Charles the Bald, the problem of Viking incursions on Frankish territories was still ever-present. In 885, a formidable fleet sailed up the Seine and the Vikings besieged Paris for approximately a year: the Parisians resisted courageously but in vain.

Whilst the Vikings who had settled in the lower Seine valley continued to persecute the inlands, Charles the Simple, crowned in 898, voluntarily negotiated with their chief, Hrólfr [Rollon], the agreement that was to constitute the very birth certificate of Normandy. It is uncertain whether Rollon was Danish or Norwegian, however, whatever his personal origins, a majority of Danish Vikings settled in what is nowadays known as Upper Normandy, a territory that they had practically kept under control over several years and that was finally conceded

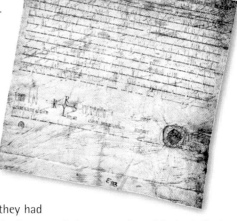

Chart of Charles the Simple dating from 918. Historical Centre of National Archives, Paris.

to them in 911 via the Treaty of Saint-Clair-sur-Epte. In exchange, they committed themselves to defending their new territories and to converting to Christianity. Rollon, who became Robert through the sacrament of baptism, far from totally deserting his Scandinavian origins, maintained a significant part of local folklore which he completed and improved with Nordic traditions. In Rouen, the Vikings did not create a Scandinavian principality, but merged with the Carolingian model.

In 924, King Raoul conceded to Rollon the region of Bayeux, where Danish colonists had settled after travelling through England. Then in 933, after the death of Rollon, Raoul conceded the Cotentin peninsula and its islands to Rollon's son, William Longsword. The north of the Cotentin region was already solidly colonised by Norwegians who had moved south from the Irish Sea, and who remained, for a long time, hostile to the new ducal authority from Rouen. Today, a place named Tingland in the headland of La Hague, reflects the probable existence of a local assembly (*þing*) in this purely Nordic zone.

The accord between the Seine Vikings and the Frankish King could have been short-lived, just like that of 921, by which, Rögnvaldr (Ragenold), chief of the Loire Vikings, obtained the county of Nantes and which turned out to be a pitiful failure. For the Vikings, who since 853 had settled

Statue of Rollon in Rouen by E. Lettelier, 1865. Museum of Normandy, Caen.

The arrival of Viking ships on the Normandy coast,
Le Petit Journal *(1911).*

in Brittany, at the mouth of the Loire and on certain coastal points, relentlessly continued their exactions until such times as Alan Barbetorte ("Twisted Beard") defeated them near Dol in 936.

On the contrary, the Treaty of Saint-Clair-sur-Epte determined a long-term policy which was extremely beneficial for Normandy, and which turned out to be one of the most durable success stories of Scandinavian colonisation throughout Christian Europe. Rollon deliberately chose integration in a region where the damage caused by the Vikings was considerable but surmountable.

Today, Normandy owes most of its originality to the Scandinavian influx on its soil. The Norse vocabulary present in modern Norman dialect, family names born from ancient Nordic forenames and totally or partially Scandinavian place names are all genuine vestiges of Normandy's Viking heritage. However, they remain almost the only tangible relics: the colonisation of Normandy was mainly characterised by the rapid and successful merger between Vikings and Franks, which, over only a few generations, gave way to that Norman people whose strength and greatness enabled William the Conqueror to challenge England.

Construction of Viking longships for William the Conqueror, according to the **Bayeux Tapestry***, 11th Century.*

the way East

Seated warriors, *Marcus Grønvold, oil on canvas, 1870, Nasjonalgalleriet Oslo.*

The Scandinavians were present in Russia for around three centuries – from 750 to 1050. They originated mainly from Sweden, but also from Denmark and Norway, were known as Varegs, and were adventurers, power-holders, merchants, slave drivers, mercenaries, farmers, politically exiled and plunderers. But whilst the western European Vikings gathered the treasures already accumulated in towns and monasteries, the Varegs organised the collection of natural riches and created exchange centres and trading routes to sell these goods.

Boat carrying, illustration from **Historia de Gentibus Septentrionalibus** *by Olaus Magnus (1490-1558), engraved wood, 16th Century. British Library, London.*

Lynx hunting, illustration from **Historia de Gentibus Septentrionalibus** *by Olaus Magnus (1490-1558), engraved wood, 16th Century.*

Volga Song, *Wassily Kandinsky,*
oil on canvas, 1944.
Centre Pompidou, National Museum of Modern Art,
Paris.

Towards Russia and the Far East, the Varegs took the same routes as their ancestors. From the depths of the Gulf of Finland, via the Neva River, then the northern Russian lakes, they joined the Don and the Dniepr towards the Black Sea to land in Constantinople. Others, from the same departure point (the current town of Saint Petersburg), followed the Volga to arrive at the north of the Caspian Sea, which they crossed towards Samarkand, Tashkent and Bukhara (Uzbekistan), and further south to Baghdad. This itinerary, whose main advantage was that it crossed the great caravan routes from the Far East, always led to the same port: Constantinople (called Miklagarõr by the Varegs) which was, at the time, the greatest city in the world.

The Baltic Sea was the central point for trade with the East. Towns such as Birka, and later Sigtuna, have preserved many vestiges of oriental imports. But the Island of Gotland is where one can find the most manifest evidence of the riches that were conveyed via this genuine internal Viking sea. For the Varegs, just like the Vikings in the West, indulged in the trade of the rarest, most precious and less cumbersome goods they could find: silk, amber, fur, textile, precious metals, arms and jewels, not forgetting the very lucrative market of slavery.

But trading was not the only incentive that led the Varegs to travel east. After having created commercial networks and drawn tributes, the Norsemen became mercenaries. Their great looks and their untameable courage made them excellent recruits for the Eastern Empire, added to the fact that they knew that, after their

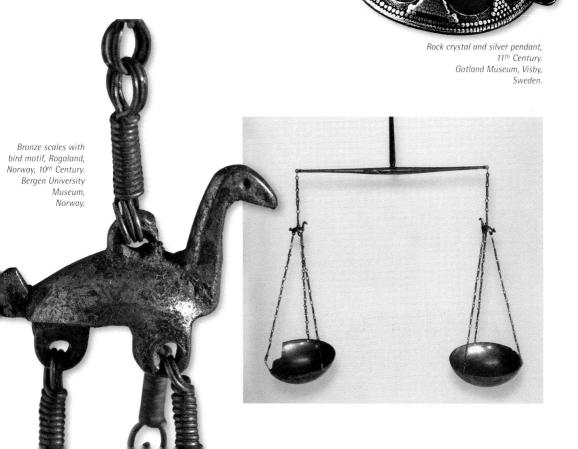

*Pendant
with bird motif, iron.
National Museum of Finland,
Helsinki.*

death, the Valkyries (Norse Goddesses) would welcome them in the *Valhöll* (hall of the slain). On the other hand, being a member of the Varingian Guard of the Emperor of Constantinople also guaranteed them prestige and riches.

Occasionally, the highest destinies awaited the Swedish Viking adventurers. *Nestor's Chronicle* recounts how, in 862, a certain number of Slavonic tribes requested that the Varegs come to restore order in their land. Led by Hrœrekr [Rurik], the Swedes, renamed the "Rús" (the name given to them by the Finish), settled in Hólmgarðr where they founded the principality of Novgorod, then in Kænugarðr [Kiev] before reorganising the country. Helgi [Oleg], Hrœrekr's successor, became king of entire Russia and chose Kiev as its capital. He developed trade, established routes and trading posts, and mounted an army for his new State with such efficiency that, in 907, he besieged Constantinople. The city had no choice but to surrender paying a phenomenal tribute. At the end of the 10th Century however, Valdemarr [Vladimir], Helgi's great grandson, married the Emperor's daughter, taking up the Christian faith at the same time and inciting, at sword point, the conversion of his troops. Hence the birth of Holy Orthodox Russia, where the Varegs were to gradually fade into the backdrop.

*Rock crystal and silver pendant,
11th Century.
Gotland Museum, Visby,
Sweden.*

*Bronze scales with
bird motif, Rogaland,
Norway, 10th Century.
Bergen University
Museum,
Norway.*

the last vikings

the christianisation of the North

Amber Cross.
Sigtuna Museum,
Sweden.

The first genuine "converter" of the North was Anschaire (Ansgar), a monk from the Abbey of Corbie in Picardy, who, as from 826, travelled to Denmark and to Sweden, whilst Anglo-Saxon missionaries preached the gospel in Norway and Iceland. The Scandinavians had for a long time frequented the Christians who were their commercial partners, and the Christian religion was by no means foreign to these Northerners, at least as from the 10th Century, and very probably beforehand. It appeared somewhat inevitable that, at the turn of the Year 1000, the North would convert to Christianity. Scandinavian countries were well aware that they could not live in autarky in any field whatsoever. And for that reason, with astonishing unanimity, they converted to Christianity together. Denmark, under the reign of King Haraldr Bluetooth did so around 960, and Iceland, after unanimous consent of the *alþing*, in 999. Norway, led by Óláfr Tryggvason, was to follow precisely in the Year 1000, and Sweden, under the reign of Olof Sköttkonungr, around 1020. This conversion of the North took place without striking a blow, without bloodshed, without "martyrs" or any other form of persecution. It should be noted that the Church was remarkably flexible, by tolerating and even encouraging for example, the engraving of runic inscriptions, erroneously considered to be magic, or by erecting churches on the very spots where the "Pagan" cult had been celebrated.

For the convert kings in each of the four Scandinavian countries, the difficulties encountered in bringing their subjects to officially accept Christianity were mainly of a political nature. For consenting to Roman, then Catholic custom implied the acceptance of a strict hierarchy, a supreme authority - the King, and the acting body that was powerfully invested in the clergy.

With the adoption of Christianity and the political view of the world that it implied, many strong kings and centralisers were

Urnes stave church, Norway.

*Haraldr Fair-Hair welcoming Guthormr, illumination from the **Flateyjarbók**, 1390. Arni Magnusson Institute, Reykjavik.*

crowned, taking example from the famous Norwegian, King Haraldr Fair-Hair, and, in particular from the Danish sovereigns. The very idea of centralisation and of hierarchical organisation, of pledging allegiance or vassalage was contradictory to the Viking mentality. It is therefore logical to consider that, within this context, Christianity was one of the major factors leading to the Viking extinction.

The sagas, a viking legacy?

Ivory liturgical comb. Sigtuna Museum, Sweden.

The end of the Viking period practically coincided with the total Christianisation of Scandinavian countries. Nevertheless, the memory of those who took to the seas in quest of glory and fortune, and of their gods, their mythology, and their royal or popular heroes was to live on to an astonishing degree. The Icelandic poets and the learned, seized by literary frenzy, and aware of the prose opportunities offered by the new Christian religion, started to write in their mother tongue, hence giving birth to one of the most astonishing cultural phenomena of the European Middle Ages.

The Eddas and Sagas, which were drafted a century and a half after the end of the Viking era, perpetuated the Viking spirit and maintained their singular vision of man, of life and of the world.

Death of Saint Olaf, *P.N. Arbo, watercolour, 1859.*
Drammen Museum, Norway.

Jet black cross,
Yorkshire
Museum.

Two very different works are nowadays known as the *Eddas*. The origin of the ancient *Edda* or the *poetic Edda*, a compilation of mythological, magical, ethical and heroic poems has long since been forgotten. Recorded in writing, at the earliest, during the 12th Century, these poems recount the great deeds of gods such as Óðinn, Þórr and Freyr, or relate great myths such as that of Sigurðr, the dragon slayer (Siegfried in Burgundian legends). The *Prose Edda*, also known as the *Snorri Edda*, owes its name to the greatest Icelandic writer of medieval times, Snorri Sturluson (1178-1241). It displays in its entirety the most complex and sophisticated poetic form that exists: that of the Norwegian Skalds, but more particularly of the Icelandic Skalds. It also elucidates a great number of myths found in the *Poetic Edda*. Why did the god Týr lose his right hand, how was poetry born, who killed Baldr, why, etc?

The Sagas, which have no cause to be jealous of our modern historical novels, are narrative prose, of varying length and often embellished with Skaldic verse. They narrate with realism, pace and even dryness, but never in lyrical mode, the life of a chosen character who, throughout his existence, has accomplished acts or deeds worthy of memory. The royal sagas are particularly worthy of mention, describing the reign of the great kings of Norway, or even of Denmark; the Icelandic sagas which recount the lives of the most famous colonisers of Iceland or of their immediate descendants; the contemporary sagas; the legendary sagas covering a genuine treasure of myths, legends and fable characters; the knights' sagas, adaptations of gestual songs or French "romans courtois". And finally, let's not forget the *þœttir* (sg. *þáttr*) which follow the same style of writing as the sagas but are always very short narrations.

The imaginary viking

During the second half of the 18th Century, the terrifying image of the Vikings and the memory of their exactions gave way to a more clement depiction of a North that more or less mingled with the Celtic world to rapidly assume a powerful image of strength and virtue. In 1750, just before James MacPherson's triumph with the Poems of Ossian, the Swiss intellectual, P.H. Mallet translated the *Edda* into French. At the dawn of roman-

Norwegian casket of Viking inspiration, given to Louis Pasteur in 1892. Institut Pasteur.

ticism, the Norsemen became the incarnation of freedom and fraternity, and were considered to be the inventors of knighthood. Chateaubriand extolled the virtues of the Viking Barbarian, bearer of a new energy that was to rejuvenate ancient and depleted civilisations. Nordic countries, far from being outshone, drew from the memory of their fierce ancestors the fabric of a national pride and a sense of identity which, even if it was to be somewhat spoilt by the hazards of history, participated in recreating an imaginary Viking and a majestic past. In 1825, from the same viewpoint, the Swedish pastor, Esaias Tegnér composed the *Frithiof's Saga* which aroused national pride among Scandinavians and which Victorian England was only too glad to adopt to eulogize its Nordic roots. However, it was not from a sense of nationalism, but from his passion for Iceland that the pre-Raphaelite, William Morris twice visited the fiery island, translated, illustrated and published several sagas. The appeal of the legendary North was also nurtured by Sabine Garing-Gould, writer and avid supernatural enthusiast, and to a lesser extent by Rudyard Kipling. And even if no Wagner opera stages Vikings per se, one cannot escape the resembling form given to the heroes and gods of the North in his Tetralogy.

Viking longship sailing to high sea,
Jean-Michel Bénier, 2004.

Taking into consideration the strong personalities of their historical and legendary characters, of their fantastic adventures and the magnificent landscapes in which they took place, the exploits of the Norsemen have not been the source of as many cinematographic works as one may expect. *The Vikings*, by Richard Fleisher (1958), remains unequalled, followed by relative successes such as *Eric the Viking* by Terry Gilliam, less inspired by the Ases (old Norse gods) than by the Knights of the Round Table, and *The 13th Warrior* inspired by the travels of Ibn Fadlan. Only a few scenes of *The Longships* by Jack Cardiff (1964) are worthy of mention, and the charm of *Prince Valiant* is mainly linked to its fidelity to the original comic strip than to an authentic Viking spirit. The magnificent *The War Lord*, by Franklin Schaffner (1965), is not intended to represent Vikings, however the Frisian pagans combine all of the characteristics of the Northern adventurers.

Siegfried et Locke, *Franz Stassen, lithography, 1914.*
Illustration for **the Niebelungen Ring.**
French National Library.

With appropriate reserve, one can also consider a few B films, either American or Italian, born during the great peplum era, and in which the flattering muscles of the kings of the seas rivalled with the scanty attire of the untameable Viking women.

In the field of comic trips, Foster created, in 1937, the unforgettable *Prince Valiant*, the 6th Century Viking and heir of Thule who fought alongside King Arthur and braved the Saxons. In turn, *Johann and Pirlouit* (Peyo), *Chevalier Ardent* (Craenhals) and *Timour* (Xavier Snoeck) all meet with the Vikings at some stage in their adventures. *Thorgal* (Rozinski and Van Hamme), although brought up by the Vikings, is a child of the stars. However, the heroine of *Yglinga Saga* by Bourgeon is a genuine Nordic princess. As for the "*Chroniques Barbares*" by Mitton, they indubitably give preference to only one aspect of the Viking adventure...

Prince Valiant, *Hal Foster. DR.*

From a humoristic point of view, Goscinny and Uderzo, who published *Asterix and the Normans* in 1967 and *Asterix and the Great Crossing* in 1975, play on anachronism with wit: "*We have not come to make war. Our descendants will look after that in a few centuries...*" exclaimed the Viking chief. But the most famous Viking of all time (with apologies to Ragnarr, Hásteinn, Leifr and the others) remains Hagar Dunor (*Hägar the Horrible*) created by Dik Browne and who, since 1973, has continued to appear in newspapers worldwide.

The world of fantasy, books, games and comic strips combined draws inspiration from the Viking warrior image just as much as from that of the Celtic hero, to create superheroes of which Conan the Cimmerian was the forerunner. Just as violent as the *berserkir*, but rarely traitors, they fill dragons with fear and walk alone towards a gloomy destiny. They trust only in their great axe and in their loyal sword or in their magico-technological equivalents.

Poster of the commemoration of the Normandy Millenium. Museum of Normandy.

Hagar Dunor,
original by Chris Browne donated to the Museum of Normandy, 1996.

pronunciation

ancient (Old Norse)		modern (Icelandic)
á	a [bat]	ao [Laos]
é	a [bait]	ié [ee-ai]
ó	o [lot]	ow [low]
u	ou [room]	u [French "u"]
ú	ou [moo]	ou [sioux]
y	u [French "u"]	i [ree]
ý	u [French "ur"]	i [ear]
œ	e [there]	ail [lie]
œ	eu [œ]	ail [lie]
ö	o [not]	eu [œ]
ø	eu [œ]	eu [œ]
au	aou [Raoul]	oy [oyai]
ei	eil [ɛj]	eil [ɛj]
ey	éu [ai-u]	eil [ɛj]
ð	th [the]	
f	f [fa] at the beginning of a word or if followed by a dull consonant; otherwise v [French "vu"]	
g	g [go] ; y [yoga] if placed before i or j	
h	h [how]	
j	y [yoga]	
p	p [pie] ; f [fa] if placed before s or t	
r	very heavily rolled	
s	ss (dull) [mass]	
þ	th (dull) [thing]	

The other vowels and consonants are pronounced as in English.

The -r ending is pronounced with a vowel similar to a French "u" (*fjörðr*), which is written in modern Icelandic: -ur (*fjörður*).

In modern language, *ll* and *rl* are pronounced dl, *rn* is pronounced dn.

All words are accentuated on the first syllable. For compound forms, the first syllable of the second word is also accentuated.

15, rue de Largerie - 14480 CULLY
Tel : 02 31 08 31 08 - Fax : 02 31 08 31 09
E-mail : info@orep-pub.com
Web : www.orep-pub.com

English translation: Heather Costil

Graphic design: OREP
ISBN : 2-915762-08-2
Copyright OREP 2006
All rights reserved
Filed officially by OREP: 1st quarter 2006
Printed in France